The Chickasaw Nation

by Karen Bush Gibson

Consultants:
Kelley Lunsford and Glenda Galvan
Division of Heritage Preservation
The Chickasaw Nation

Bridgestone Books
an imprint of Capstone Press
Mankato, Minnesota

Bridgestone Books are published by Capstone Press
151 Good Counsel Drive, P.O. Box 669, Mankato, Minnesota 56002
http://www.capstone-press.com

Library of Congress Cataloging-in-Publication Data
Gibson, Karen Bush.
   The Chickasaw Nation/by Karen Bush Gibson.
      p. cm.—(Native peoples)
      Summary: Provides an overview of the past and present lives of the Chickasaw
people, covering their history, daily lives and activities, customs, family life, religion,
and government. Includes instructions for making a shell shaker and a gorget to be
worn when dancing.
      Includes bibliographical references and index.
      ISBN 0-7368-1365-9 (hardcover)
      1. Chickasaw Indians—Juvenile literature. [1. Chickasaw Indians.
2. Indians of North America—Oklahoma.] I. Title. II. Series.
E99.C55 G53 2003
976′.004973—dc21
                                                                2002000013

Editorial Credits
Rebecca Glaser, editor; Karen Risch, product planning editor; Heidi Meyer, book designer
      and illustrator; Alta Schaffer, photo researcher

Photo Credits
Chickasaw Division of Heritage Preservation/American Museum of Natural History, 20
Chickasaw Division of Heritage Preservation, donated by Lorie Robins, 6
Gerrell Newby, Chickasaw Nation, cover, 10, 14
Janet McCoy, Chickasaw Division of Heritage Preservation, 8, 12
Marie Gibson, Chickasaw Division of Heritage Preservation, 16
Tom Phillips, Chickasaw Division of Heritage Preservation, 18

1 2 3 4 5 6 07 06 05 04 03 02

Table of Contents

The Chickasaw once lived and hunted in what is now the southeastern United States. The yellow region shows the lands the Chickasaw lost in treaties. Today, their tribal headquarters is in southern Oklahoma.

Fast Facts

The Chickasaw (chah-KAH-shah) people of south-central Oklahoma are known as one of the Five Civilized Tribes. The Cherokee, Chickasaw, Choctaw, Creek, and Seminole are five tribes that adopted many European ways. These facts tell about the Chickasaw in the past and today.

Homes: In the past, Chickasaws built summer and winter houses from logs, clay, cane, grass, and bark. Today, the Chickasaws live in modern homes and apartments.

Food: Chickasaws once hunted and gathered food from forests. They also grew corn, beans, and squash. Today, Chickasaw people buy food in grocery stores.

Clothing: Long ago, Chickasaws wore clothing made from animal skins. Winter robes of animal fur kept them warm. Chickasaws now wear modern clothing. Some Chickasaws might wear traditional clothing for special gatherings.

Language: The Chickasaw language comes from the Muskogean group of languages. American Indians in the southeastern United States spoke Muskogean languages. In the 1700s, Chickasaw was the language used by traders along the lower Mississippi River.

The Hamilton family of Chickasaws lived in Indian Territory.
This photo was taken in about 1900.

6

History

The Chickasaws were great warriors. Few other tribes could beat them. Chickasaws often attacked other tribes and took slaves.

In 1540, Spanish explorer Hernando de Soto was the first European to meet the Chickasaws. For 200 years, Europeans fought for control of the Southeast. Spain, France, and England each wanted the help of American Indians. The Chickasaws helped the English defeat the French.

In the late 1700s, many settlers arrived in Chickasaw lands. Their land included parts of what is now Mississippi, Tennessee, Kentucky, and Alabama.

The Indian Removal Act of 1830 forced American Indians to move west. The Chickasaws lost much of their land through treaties with the U.S. government. The Chickasaws were the last nation to move to Indian Territory in what is now Oklahoma. Their journey to Indian Territory is called the Trail of Tears. Many people died on the way. By 1845, most Chickasaws had moved.

8

The Chickasaw People

Today, the Chickasaw Nation has about 42,000 members. Many of them live in Oklahoma. But Chickasaws live all over the world. Their tribal headquarters is in Ada, Oklahoma.

Chicasha is the nation's name for itself. It means "he who walked away."

Today, many Chickasaws speak only English. Some Chickasaw people want to learn more about traditional ways. Elders teach Chickasaw language classes. Some Chickasaws learn traditional crafts such as beadwork and finger weaving. This type of weaving is done all by hand. Chickasaw artists and craftspeople display their work all around the United States.

Another way Chickasaw people celebrate their past is by holding traditional stomp dances. Chickasaws get together to dance and sing at these events. Some people wear traditional clothing to stomp dances.

Chickasaw women weave belts and other items by hand. Finger weaving is a traditional Chickasaw craft.

This modern model of a Chickasaw winter house
shows its traditional round shape.

Homes, Food, and Clothing

Early Chickasaw families had homes for different seasons. The winter house was made from logs. Chickasaws put a mixture of clay and dried grass between the logs to keep the house warm. Summer houses were rectangular. The walls were made of woven mats that let air through to keep the houses cool. By the 1850s, most Chickasaws lived in log cabins. Today, Chickasaws live in modern homes and apartments.

In the past, Chickasaws hunted deer and other animals. They also grew squash, corn, and beans. Today, Chickasaw people buy food at grocery stores.

Long ago, Chickasaws wore deerskin clothing. Robes of bison, panther, bear, and otter skins kept people warm in winter. After Europeans came, many men wore cloth shirts, trader's pants, and straw hats. Women wore cotton dresses. Clothing was decorated with feathers, beadwork, or shells. Today, Chickasaws wear modern clothes.

The Chickasaw Family

The Chickasaws once lived in large family groups called clans. A husband and wife came from different clans. Their children belonged to the mother's clan. A mother's brothers taught boys about hunting and being warriors. The mother taught girls about cooking, sewing, and gardening. Women also could be warriors. A woman warrior's clan cared for her children when she was at war.

Chickasaws respect their elders. Elders have the most knowledge because they have lived the longest. They may help raise children. Elders also teach young people about Chickasaw language and culture.

The Chickasaws no longer live in clans. But family still is important. The people of the nation believe there should be no lost children. When parents cannot raise a child, the grandparents or someone else in the nation cares for the child.

Chickasaw young people enjoy listening to their elders.

Chickasaw Government

The Chickasaw tribe always has had a democratic government. In a democracy, all people have a voice in decisions that affect the nation.

Long ago, clans were ruled by a council of elders and a chief, or minko (MIN-ko). Each clan council and chief reported to the high minko. The high minko was in charge of the entire nation.

The war chief was second in command to the high minko. A war chief planned when and where to make attacks. Tishomingo was the last war chief. He died during the Trail of Tears. The historic Chickasaw capitol in Oklahoma is named after him.

The Chickasaw government today works like many state governments. Since 1971, the Chickasaw people have elected a governor and lieutenant governor every four years. The Chickasaw also elect 13 legislators to make laws. Three judges sit on the Chickasaw Supreme Court. They make decisions on tribal cases.

The Chickasaw built the Tishomingo Capitol in 1898 for government offices. They are now restoring the building to its original look for a museum.

Chickasaw Religion

The Chickasaws always have believed in a supreme being. Long ago, this being was called Ababinili. This name means "he who lives above the heavens."

Ceremonies are an important part of Chickasaw religion. One past ceremony was the Green Corn ceremony, held in late summer when the corn ripened. The Green Corn ceremony was a time of forgiveness and renewal. People made promises for the coming year. The ceremony ended with feasting and dancing.

Today, Chickasaws practice ceremonial song and dance. Their ancient songs tell about families, stories, nature, and surroundings.

In the early 1800s, missionaries taught Chickasaws about Christianity. Christians follow the teachings of Jesus Christ. The missionaries helped build tribal schools. Today, many Chickasaws follow the Christian religion. Chickasaw church services may be in the Chickasaw language.

Chickasaws made pashofa during the Green Corn ceremony. This dish is made from cracked corn and pork. Today, Chickasaws make pashofa for big events.

Migration Story

Long ago, the Chickasaw and Choctaw were one nation. They did not always live in the southeastern United States. The people wanted a new home and asked Ababinili for help. Ababinili sent them a sacred pole. After traveling each day, the people stuck the pole in the ground. The pole would lean in one direction. Each morning, the people traveled in the direction the pole leaned.

Both groups followed the sacred pole east. When the pole was in what is now Mississippi, it wobbled and then stopped in a straight position. Choctaw and his followers believed they should stop traveling and settle there. Chickasaw and his people believed they should continue. The Chickasaws continued following the pole in the direction it wobbled. They stopped near the present-day town of Tupelo, Mississippi.

Chickasaw and Choctaw, the two brothers, disagreed when the sacred pole wobbled. Chickasaw (right) thought his group should keep going.

Oral Tradition

The Chickasaw people have a long history of oral tradition. Stories explained things about the world. The stories also taught lessons about life. Chickasaws did not write down stories. Elders told them to younger people.

Chickasaw storytellers tell many stories about animals and nature. There are also legends about Invisible Little People, How Poison Came to the World, and the Great Flood.

One story tells about Sinti-Holo, the sacred snake. Most people could not see this horned snake. A boy sometimes would get close enough to see one. People believed boys who saw the snake would become wise men.

Te Ata Fisher (1895–1995) was a famous Chickasaw storyteller. She traveled all over the world telling stories. She was asked to share her stories with President Franklin Roosevelt and his wife Eleanor.

Te Ata Fisher was a Chickasaw woman who told traditional stories.

Hands On: Stomp Dance Wear

At stomp dances, women wear shell shakers on their legs. Shell shakers are made by putting pebbles inside turtle shells. Men wear a silver gorget (GOR-jet) around their neck. You can make samples of these items from paper plates.

Shell Shaker (girls)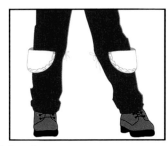

Gorget (boys)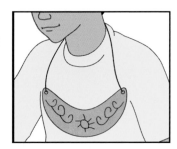

What You Need

Small paper plate
About 15 uncooked beans or
    unpopped popcorn
Stapler
Hole punch
Yarn

What You Do

1. Fold the paper plate in half. Fill it with uncooked beans or popcorn.
2. Staple the opening closed.
3. Using a hole punch, put a hole in both corners.
4. Thread yarn through both holes. Tie the shell shaker to your leg below the knee.

What You Need

Small paper plate
Scissors
Aluminum foil
Markers
Hole punch
Yarn

What You Do

1. Cut out a crescent moon shape from a paper plate to make the gorget.
2. Wrap aluminum foil around the gorget. Draw designs on it.
3. Punch a hole in both corners.
4. Tie two pieces of yarn to each hole. Tie the gorget loosely around the front of your neck.

Words to Know

cane (KANE)—the woody, hollow stem of the sugarcane plant; the Chickasaw used cane for building houses.

civilized (SIV-i-lizd)—educated and well-mannered

council (KOUN-suhl)—a group of leaders chosen to look after the interests of a community

culture (KUHL-chur)—the ideas, traditions, and ways of life of a group of people

migration (mye-GRAY-shun)—a journey in which people leave one area and settle in another

missionary (MISH-uh-nair-ee)—someone who is sent by a church to teach that church's beliefs

trader's pants (TRAY-durz PANTS)—cloth pants from European traders

traditional (truh-DISH-uhn-uhl)—using the styles, manners, and ways of the past

treaty (TREE-tee)—a formal agreement between two or more governments or nations

Read More

Ansary, Mir Tamim. *Southeast Indians.* Native Americans. Des Plaines, Ill.: Heinemann Library, 2000.

Lassieur, Allison. *The Choctaw Nation.* Native Peoples. Mankato, Minn.: Bridgestone Books, 2001.

Useful Addresses

**The Chickasaw Nation
   Tribal Library**
P.O. Box 1548
Ada, OK 74821-1548

**Chickasaw Nation Visitor
   Center**
520 East Arlington Boulevard
Ada, OK 74821

Internet Sites

Chickasaw Nation
http://www.chickasaw.net

Index of Native American Resources on the Internet
http://www.hanksville.org/NAresources

Index